Introduction

Presenting Poetry provides the basis of a number of poetry sessions for primary classes (approximately 8- to 12-year-olds). The units contain:

1. a group of poems linked by a common theme, structure or feature;
2. some questions about the poems, designed to help pupils get the most out of their reading;
3. one or more follow-up activities, for example art or craft work, drama, discussion, music, recitation, choral presentation or poetry writing. These activities are often non-written and intended to show poetry as linked to the aesthetic and expressive arts.

A typical poetry session might take the following shape:

1. re-reading together of a poem or poems enjoyed in a previous session;
2. time for pupils to choose and read for pleasure, with the group, some of their favourite poems;
3. a detailed look at one unit, and follow-up work related to it. The book can, of course, also be used more informally in odd moments as a poetry anthology.

Reading the poems

When pupils meet each poem for the first time, it should be through the teacher's reading, because a well-read rendering maximises the listener's pleasure. It is strongly recommended, therefore, that teachers *practise* each poem before reading it aloud for the first time to the class. Later on, the pupils should have an opportunity to read aloud themselves. If the teacher has provided a good example of how to handle rhythm, rhyme, dramatic effects, etc., the pupil's task will be easier and more pleasurable. The pupil will also have been introduced to new or difficult words or ideas.

After this first teacher-reading of the poem, the pupil's understanding should be ensured through discussion based on the comprehension questions in the text. A second teacher-reading of the poem is often a good idea, before handing over to pupil-readers.

Although comprehension questions are included, full comprehension by all pupils of all poems is not always possible – nor is it essential. Children are well used to coping with half-grasped ideas, and may enjoy the sounds and images of the more difficult poems for their own sake.

It is recommended that all pupil-readers be volunteers and that no pupil be forced to read. It is best to choose competent volunteers first and less competent ones later on when they have had a chance to become more familiar with words and rhythms from several hearings. It is worth trying a wide range of reading methods: single voice reading, paired reading, group reading, choral reading, and combinations of these. Happy chanting (where appropriate) is not to be despised: it gives pleasure and helps commit poems to memory. When possible and practical, children may be encouraged to use sound effects, music, etc., to accompany their readings.

Follow-up

Any follow-up work should be varied and pleasurable. Some poetry writing is included as part of a balanced follow-up programme. Unit poems are often used as a model for the pupil's work, since this is an effective way of starting children off on their own poetry writing. Learning poetry by heart is a useful memory-training exercise and can provide great pleasure. Children should be encouraged to learn their favourite poems by heart every now and then. Often poems are picked up effortlessly if they are read aloud frequently. The prospect of an audience motivates children's performance enormously. Try to provide an audience – another class, the school – for their presentations.

Contents

PRESENTING
POETRY 3

PATRICIA McCALL, SUE PALMER
AND GORDON JARVIE

Hodder & Stoughton
A MEMBER OF THE HODDER HEADLINE GROUP

Illustrations by Ian Andrew, Shirley Bellwood, Linda Birch, Francis Blake, Margaret Chamberlain, Rowan Clifford, John Fardell, Sheila Galbraith, John Harrold, Thelma Lambert, John Marshall, Steve Smallman and Guy Smith

First edition published 1986 by Oliver & Boyd

British Library Cataloguing in Publication Data
A catalogue record for this title is available from The British Library

ISBN 0 340 67007 X

First published 1986 by Oliver & Boyd
Revised edition 1996 Hodder & Stoughton
Impression number   10   9   8   7   6   5   4   3   2   1
Year   1999   1988   1997   1996

Typeset by Hewer Text Composition Services, Edinburgh.
Printed in Hong Kong for Hodder & Stoughton Educational, a division of Hodder Headline Plc, 338 Euston Road, London NW1 3BH by Colorcraft Ltd, Hong Kong.

Monsters

The Marrog

My desk's at the back of the class
And nobody, nobody knows
I'm a Marrog from Mars
With a body of brass
And seventeen fingers and toes.
Wouldn't they shriek if they knew
I've three eyes at the back of my head
And my hair is bright purple
My nose is deep blue
And my teeth are half yellow, half red?
My five arms are silver, and spiked
With knives on them sharper than spears.
I could go back right now if I liked –
And return in a million light years.
I could gobble them all,
For I'm seven foot tall
And I'm breathing green flame from my ears.
Wouldn't they yell if they knew,
If they guessed that a Marrog was here?
Ha-ha they haven't a clue –
Or wouldn't they tremble with fear!
"Look, look, a Marrog"
They'd all scream — and SMACK
The blackboard would fall and the ceiling would crack
And the teacher would faint, I suppose.
But I grin to myself, sitting right at the back
And nobody, nobody knows.

R. C. Scriven

Is there really a Marrog at the back of the class? Why do you give that answer?

The next poem is about a mythical sea-monster, which is mentioned in the Bible.

Leviathan

God's deathless plaything rolls an eye
Five hundred thousand cubits high.
The smallest scale upon his tail.
Could hide six dolphins and a whale.
His nostrils breathe, and on the spot
The churning waves turn seething hot.
If he be hungry, one huge fin
Drives seven thousand fishes in;
And when he drinks what he may need,
The rivers of the earth recede.
Yet he is more than huge and strong—
Twelve brilliant colours play along
His sides until, compared to him,
The naked, burning sun seems dim.

Louis Untermeyer

A cubit – the distance from one's elbow to one's finger-tips.

Leviathan is enormously big. Which parts of the poem show you this? Can you think of anything else as big as Leviathan?

The next poem comes from Australia, and mentions some people and animals from there:

bunyip – a mythical Australian monster
kookaburra – an Australian bird
abo – short for Aborigine, one of the native people of Australia
yabbie – a small crayfish

Every second verse in *The Bunyip* is the bunyip actually talking. All the other verses describe the strange Australian landscape.

The Bunyip

The water down the rocky wall
Lets fall its shining stair;
The bunyip in the deep green pool
Looks up it to the air.

The kookaburra drank, he says, then shrieked at me with laughter,
I dragged him down in a hairy hand and ate his thighbones after–
My head is bruised with the falling foam, the water blinds my eye,
Yet I will climb that waterfall and walk upon the sky.

The turpentine and stringybark,
The dark red bloodwoods lean
And drop their shadows in the pool
With blue sky in between.

A beast am I, the bunyip says, my voice a drowning cow's.
Yet am I not a singing bird among these waving boughs?
I raise my black and dripping head, I cry a bubbling cry;
For I shall climb the trunks of trees to walk upon the sky.

Gold and red the gum-trees glow,
Yellow gleam the ferns;
The bunyip in the crimson pool
Believes the water burns.

I know the roots of rocks, he says, I know the door of hell;
I ate the abo's daughter once, I know my faults full well;
Yet sunset walks between the trees and sucks the water dry,
And when the whole world's burnt away I'll walk upon the sky.

The little frogs they call like bells,
The bunyip swims alone;
Across the pool the stars are laid
Like stone by silver stone.

What did I do before I was born, the bunyip asks the night;
I looked at myself in the water's glass and I nearly died of fright;
Condemned to haunt a pool in the bush while a thousand years go by—
Yet I walk on the stars like stepping-stones and I'll climb them into the sky.

A lady walks across the night
And sees that mirror there;
Oh, is it for herself alone
The moon lets down her hair?

The yabbie's back is green for her, his claws are opal-blue,
Look for my soul, the bunyip says, for it was a jewel too.
I bellowed with woe to the yabbie once, but all I said was a lie,
For I'll catch the moon by her silver hair and dance her around the sky.

Douglas Stewart

7

Where does the Bunyip live?
How big do you think he is? Why?
Look through the poem to find some other clues to what the Bunyip looks like.
Do you think he is happy about the way he looks? Why?
Why do you think he wants *to walk upon the sky*?
The poem can be read in two voices. One voice reads the shorter stanzas which describe the landscape. The other reads the longer stanzas where the Bunyip is speaking.
What sort of expression do you feel the Buynip ought to have in his voice? Fierce? Gentle? Cruel? Angry? Sad?
Discuss this before some pairs of people read the poem aloud again.

ACTIVITY: **Monster Pictures**

Try making a picture of a Monster. You could choose one of the monsters in the poem or invent your own.
Start with paint or crayon, and then use pictures cut from magazines, foil or anything else you can find to add extra monstrous bits. Make it as scary and peculiar as you can.

UNIT TWO

East is East

This unit is about the poetry of China and Japan.

Chinese Poetry
Writers have been composing poetry in China for more than three thousand years. Often Chinese poems are short, sad thoughts about being separated from loved ones. The first poem is one like this. It is a very famous poem written by Li Po, a poet who lived twelve hundred years ago. Li Po sets his poem against the backdrop of Nature – this is very common in Chinese writing.

Quiet Night Thoughts

Before my bed
there is bright moonlight
So that it seems
like frost on the ground:

Lifting my head
I watch the bright moon,
Lowering my head
I dream that I'm home.

translated by Arthur Cooper

Do you like this poem? Why do you feel as you do?
Does the poet succeed in painting a picture in your mind with his words? If he does, try to describe what you can see in your mind's eye. How do you picture the room and the poet? You might like to look up a book on Ancient China to find out what houses, furnishings and clothing were like in Li Po's time.

The next poem was written by a Chinese princess many hundreds of years ago.
Poor Hsi-Chun was sent away from her happy home in a civilised Chinese city to marry a strange barbarian chief – the king of the nomadic Wu-Sun tribe. She was probably very young when she was sent far away from her home and her family, never to return...

The Lament of Hsi-Chun

My people have married me
In a far corner of Earth:
Sent me away to a strange land,
To the king of the Wu-Sun.
A tent is my house,
Of felt are my walls;
Raw flesh my food
With mare's milk to drink.
Always thinking of my own country,
My heart sad within,
Would I were a yellow stork
And could fly to my old home!

translated by Arthur Waley

Why do you think Hsi-Chun was made to marry the king of the Wu-Sun? What things seem strange to her in her new life?
Have you ever spent time away from home?
What seemed different and unfamiliar to you?
Did you ever get used to these things?
Do you think Hsi-Chun ever got used to the felt walls and nasty food?

10

The last two poems have been rather sad, but not all Chinese poems are sad.
The next one is light-hearted and is about going bald, of all things. It was written by Po Chu-i who lived shortly after Li Po.

On His Baldness

At dawn I sighed to see my hairs fall
At dusk I sighed to see my hairs fall.
For I dreaded the time when the last lock should go. . .
They are all gone and I do not mind at all!
I have done with that cumbrous washing and getting dry;
My tiresome comb for ever is laid aside.
Best of all, when the weather is hot and wet,
To have no top-knot weighing down on one's head!

I put aside my messy cloth wrap;
I have got rid of my dusty tasselled fringe.
In a silver jar I have stored a cold stream,
On my bald pate I trickle a ladle full.
Like one baptised with the water of Buddha's Law,
I sit and receive this cool, cleansing joy.
Now I know why the priest who seeks Repose
Frees his heart by first shaving his head.

translated by Arthur Waley

Why does the poet like being bald after all? Do you think doing without hair sounds like a good idea?
Are there any ''grooming'' routines in your life that you find a chore and would like to be rid of? What about grown-ups? Do you think men like shaving every morning? Do you think women like putting on make-up?

Japanese Haiku

This section of the unit concentrates on one particular type of *Japanese* poetry – *haiku*. Haiku are very short poems which follow a set pattern. They have three lines with an exact number of syllables in each line, for example:

> ✓ ✓ ✓ ✓ ✓
> How bright the rainbow   5
> ✓ ✓ ✓ ✓ ✓✓ ✓
> Lighting the far horizon   7
> ✓ ✓ ✓ ✓ ✓
> Scattering rain clouds.   5

The syllable pattern 5,7,5 is marked, with each syllable shown by a ✓ sign above it.
Tap out and count the syllables in each line. This 5,7,5 syllable pattern is the traditional form of the Japanese haiku.
Practise tapping and counting out the names of some people in your class to see how many syllables each one has.

> ✓ ✓ ✓   ✓ ✓ ✓ ✓ ✓
> e.g. **Daniel Hall**   **Lucy Alexander**

Now look at the next haiku and notice the same 5,7,5 pattern.

> ✓✓ ✓ ✓ ✓
> Spiders' webs shimmer   5
> ✓ ✓ ✓ ✓ ✓ ✓ ✓
> Breath billows out like snow clouds   7
> ✓ ✓ ✓ ✓ ✓
> White, frosted morning.   5

The syllables are not marked in the next one. Read the haiku and count them for yourself.

> Cat stretches slowly
> Pads into the night garden
> Shiver, small creatures!

This syllable pattern is only one of the special features of the haiku. Here are some others:

1. Haiku are usually about Nature.
2. The last line of a haiku usually ends in a noun.
3. The last line of a haiku often either makes a contrast with what is in the first two lines, or trails gently away leaving the reader thinking. . .
4. Haiku are thoughtful little poems, often rather sad and haunting.

ACTIVITY: **Haiku Writing**

Use the haiku in the unit as models and try to write some of your own. Remember all the special features of the haiku which are mentioned in the unit. When your haiku are finished, you might like to illustrate them and make a class book.
If you are thinking of an idea, it may help to look out of the classroom window at the sky, the weather or any greenery and living creatures that may be visible. You may also find an idea if you think back to the last time you were in the country or by the sea. Pets can also be a good subject to write about.

Mysteries

Who do you think Lulu is? Who is the person talking?
What do *you* think has happened to Lulu?
Read the poem a few times. There are plenty of clues to Lulu's disappearance.
Can you find an answer to the mystery which fits in exactly with the poem?

What has happened to Lulu?

What has happened to Lulu, mother?
  What has happened to Lu?
There's nothing in her bed but an old rag-doll
  And by its side a shoe.

Why is her window wide, mother,
  The curtain flapping free,
And only a circle on the dusty shelf
  Where her money-box used to be?

Why do you turn your head, mother,
  And why do the tear-drops fall?
And why do you crumple that note on the fire
  And say it is nothing at all?

I woke to voices late last night,
  I heard an engine roar.
Why do you tell me the things I heard
  Were a dream and nothing more?

I heard somebody cry, mother,
  In anger or in pain,
But now I ask you why, mother,
  You say it was a gust of rain.

Why do you wander about as though
  You don't know what to do?
What has happened to Lulu, mother?
  What has happened to Lu?

Charles Causley

The next poem is about a true incident.
Some years ago three lighthouse keepers
vanished mysteriously from Flannan Isle, a tiny
remote island far out in the Atlantic, off the West
Coast of Scotland. Nobody else lived on the
island, so there were no witnesses to say what
happened to them. The three men were
experienced lighthouse keepers who knew that,
whatever disaster might befall, they must never
allow the lamp to go out. To ensure that this did
not happen, they were expected never to leave
the lighthouse unattended . . . but they did.
The poem begins with the approach to Flannan
Isle of a rescue ship which has been sent to
discover why the lighthouse lamp has gone
out.

Flannan Isle

Though three men dwell on Flannan Isle
To keep the lamp alight,
As we steered under the lee we caught
No glimmer through the night.

A passing ship at dawn had brought
The news, and quickly we set sail,
To find out what strange thing might ail
The keepers of the deep-sea light.

The winter day broke blue and bright
With glancing sun and glancing spray
While o'er the swell our boat made way,
As gallant as a gull in flight.

But as we neared the lonely Isle
And looked up at the naked height,
And saw the lighthouse towering white
With blinded lantern that all night
Had never shot a spark
Of comfort through the dark,
So ghostly in the cold sunlight
It seemed that we were struck the while
With wonder all too dread for words.

And, as into the tiny creek
We stole beneath the hanging crag,
We saw three queer black ugly birds—
Too big by far in my belief,
For cormorant or shag—
Like seamen sitting bolt-upright
Up on a half-tide reef:
But, as we neared, they plunged from sight
Without a sound or spurt of white.

And still too mazed to speak,
We landed; and made fast the boat;
And climbed the track in single file,
Each wishing he was safe afloat
On any sea, however far,
So be it far from Flannan Isle:
And still we seemed to climb and climb
As though we'd lost all count of time
And so must climb for evermore.
Yet, all too soon, we reached the door—
The black, sun-blistered lighthouse-door,
That gaped for us ajar.

As on the threshold for a spell
We paused, we seemed to breathe the smell
Of limewash and of tar,
Familiar as our daily breath,
As though 'twere some strange scent of death;
And so yet wondering, side by side
We stood a moment still tongue-tied;
And each with black foreboding eyed
The door, ere we should fling it wide
To leave the sunlight for the gloom:
Till, plucking courage up, at last
Hard on each other's heels we passed
Into the living room.

Yet as we crowded through the door
We only saw a table spread
For dinner, meat and cheese and bread;
But all untouched and no-one there:
As though when they sat down to eat,
Ere they could even taste,
Alarm had come; and they in haste
Had risen and left the bread and meat,
For at the table-head a chair
Lay tumbled on the floor.

We listened, but we only heard
The feeble chirping of a bird
That starved upon its perch;
And, listening still, without a word
We set about our hopeless search.
We hunted high, we hunted low,
And soon ransacked the empty house;
Then o'er the Island, to and fro
We ranged, to listen and to look

15

In every cranny, cleft or nook
That might have hid a bird or mouse:
But though we searched from shore to shore
We found no sign in any place,
And soon again stood face to face
Before the gaping door,
And stole into the room once more
As frightened children steal.

Ay, though we hunted high and low
And hunted everywhere,
Of the three men's fate we found no trace
Of any kind in any place
But a door ajar, and an untouched meal,
And an overtoppled chair.

And as we listened in the gloom
Of that forsaken living-room—
A chill clutch on our breath—
We thought how ill-chance came to all
Who kept the Flannan Light,
And how the rock had been the death
Of many a likely lad—
How six had come to a sudden end
And three had gone stark mad,
And one whom we'd all known as friend,
Had leapt from the lantern one still night,
And fallen dead by the lighthouse wall—
And long we thought
On the three we sought,
And on what might yet befall.

Like curs a glance has brought to heel
We listened, flinching there,

And looked and looked on the untouched meal,
And the overtoppled chair.

We seemed to stand for an endless while,
Though still no word was said,
Three men alive on Flannan Isle
Who thought on three men dead.

Wilfrid Wilson Gibson

What clues are there about what happened to
the three men?
What hints in the poem seem to suggest a
supernatural explanation?
What do you think happened on Flannan Isle?
Do you think there was a natural explanation
or do you think something supernatural
happened?

The last poem is about an imaginary
mysterious incident.

The Listeners

'Is there anybody there?' said the Traveller,
  Knocking on the moonlit door;
And his horse in the silence champed the grasses
  Of the forest's ferny floor:

And a bird flew up out of the turret,
  Above the Traveller's head:
And he smote upon the door again a second time;
  'Is there anybody there?' he said.
But no one descended to the Traveller;
  No head from the leaf-fringed sill
Leaned over and looked into his grey eyes,
  Where he stood perplexed and still.
But only a host of phantom listeners
  That dwelt in the lone house then
Stood listening in the quiet of the moonlight
  To that voice from the world of men:
Stood thronging the faint moonbeams on the dark stair,
  That goes down to the empty hall,
Hearkening in an air stirred and shaken
  By the lonely Traveller's call.
And he felt in his heart their strangeness,
  Their stillness answering his cry,
While his horse moved, cropping the dark turf,
  'Neath the starred and leafy sky;
For he suddenly smote on the door, even
  Louder, and lifted his head:—
'Tell them I came, and no one answered,
  That I kept my word,' he said.
Never the least stir made the listeners,
  Though every word he spake
Fell echoing through the shadowiness of the still house
  From the one man left awake:
Ay, they heard his foot upon the stirrup,
  And the sound of iron on stone,
And how the silence surged softly backward,
  When the plunging hoofs were gone.

Walter De La Mare

The Listeners is really like the last act of a play or the last chapter of a book. It tells the end of the story, but not the beginning.
How do you think the story might have started? Why did the traveller make a promise to return? To whom did he make the promise? Why had things changed in the *lone house* by the time he did return?

Rosen and McGough

Michael Rosen and Roger McGough are two popular British poets. They have both appeared often on television, so you may have seen them.

Michael Rosen writes poems mainly for young people. He is very good at noticing annoying things about adults:

Michael Rosen

Chivvy

Grown-ups say things like:
Speak up
Don't talk with your mouth full
Don't stare
Don't point
Don't pick your nose
Sit up
Say please
Less noise
Shut the door behind you
Don't drag your feet
Haven't you got a hankie?
Take your hands out of your pockets
Pull your socks up
Stand up straight
Say thank you
Don't interrupt
No one thinks you're funny
Take your elbows off the table
Can't you make your *own*
mind up about anything?

Michael Rosen

Michael Rosen lives in London, and can sometimes be seen running around Hackney Marshes, trying to keep fit. He often visits schools to talk about poetry and recite some of his poems to the classes he meets. You can tell that he remembers his own schooldays:

Rodge Said

Rodge said,
'Teachers—they want it all ways—
You're jumping up and down on a chair
or something
and they grab hold of you and say,
"Would you do that sort of thing in your own home?"

'So you say, "No."
And they say,
"Well don't do it here then."

'But if you say, "Yes, I do it at home."
they say,
"Well, we don't want that sort of thing
going on here
thank you very much."

'Teachers – they get you all ways,'
Rodge said.

Michael Rosen

Try reading Michael Rosen's poems aloud yourself. The reading voice of *Chivvy* can sound like all the nagging grown-ups you know.
In *Rodge Said*, Rodge should sound fed up and the teacher very school-marmy.

Roger McGough

Roger McGough is older than Michael Rosen. His poems are not usually written specially for young people, but they are often funny and entertaining – like this teacher's dream of revenge on his class.

The Lesson

A poem that raises the question:
Should there be capital punishment in schools?

Chaos ruled OK in the classroom
as bravely the teacher walked in
the nooligans ignored him
his voice was lost in the din

'The theme for today is violence
and homework will be set
I'm going to teach you a lesson
one that you'll never forget'

He picked on a boy who was shouting
and throttled him then and there
then garrotted the girl behind him
(the one with grotty hair)

Then sword in hand he hacked his way
between the chattering rows
'First come, first severed' he declared
'fingers, feet, or toes'

He threw the sword at a latecomer
it struck with deadly aim
then pulling out a shotgun
he continued with his game

The first blast cleared the backrow
(where those who skive hang out)
they collapsed like rubber dinghies
when the plug's pulled out

'Please may I leave the room sir?'
a trembling vandal enquired
'Of course you may' said teacher
put the gun to his temple and fired

The Head popped a head round the doorway
to see why a din was being made
nodded understandingly
then tossed in a grenade

And when the ammo was well spent
with blood on every chair
Silence shuffled forward
with its hands up in the air

The teacher surveyed the carnage
the dying and the dead
He waggled a finger severely
'Now let that be a lesson' he said.

Roger McGough

What sort of revenge might people in other jobs take? What about a dustman? A school dinner lady? The Queen?

'The Fight of the Year'

'And there goes the bell for the third month
and Winter comes out of its corner looking groggy
Spring leads with a left to the head
followed by a sharp right to the body
  daffodils
  primroses
  crocuses
  snowdrops

lilacs
violets
pussywillow
Winter can't take much more punishment
and Spring shows no signs of tiring
tadpoles
squirrels
baalambs
badgers
bunny rabbits
mad march hares
horses and hounds
Spring is merciless
Winter won't go the full twelve rounds
bobtail clouds
scallywaggy winds
the sun
a pavement artist
in every town
A left to the chin
and Winter's down!
tomatoes
radish
cucumber
onions
beetroot
celery
and any
amount
of lettuce
for dinner
Winter's out for the count
Spring is the winner!'

Roger McGough

Roger McGough used to be in a pop group called Scaffold, which had several hit records. Now he mainly writes and recites his poems.

The poems in this unit come from *You Tell Me* (Puffin), by McGough and Rosen. The poem on the front cover of this book is also from *You Tell Me*.

ACTIVITY: **Drama**

Read '*The Fight of the Year*' again. Go into groups of about four and work out a good way of presenting this poem on tape.
Some things to think about:
What sort of voice does a sports commentator use?
What does the referee start to do as soon as a boxer is knocked down?
What does it mean when a boxer is "counted out"?
What sort of sound effects could you have in the background?
When your teacher calls you together, some groups could give their presentations, and perhaps put them on tape for another class to hear.

Here Lie the Bones...

An epitaph is what is written on somebody's gravestone. Usually epitaphs are solemn and sad, but in the past there have been some very funny ones.

In Memory of
THOMAS THETCHER
a Grenadier in the North Reg.t
of Hants Militia, who died of a
violent Fever contracted by drinking
Small Beer when hot the 12th of May
1764, Aged 26 Years.

In grateful remembrance of whose universal
good will towards his Comrades, this Stone
is placed here at their expence, as a small
testimony of their regard and concern;

Here sleeps in peace a Hampshire Grenadier,
Who caught his death by drinking cold small Beer,
Soldiers be wise from his untimely fall
And when ye're hot drink Strong or none at all.

This memorial being decay'd was restor'd
by the Officers of the Garrison A.D. 1781,

An honest Soldier never is forgot,
Whether he die by Musket or by Pot.

This Stone was placed by the North Hants
Militia, when disembodied at Winchester
on 26th April 1802, in consequence of
the original Stone being destroyed.

Poor Martha Snell, she's gone away—
She would if she could but she couldn't stay.
She'd two bad legs and a baddish cough
But it was her legs that carried her off.

Here lies the body of Michael Shay
Who died maintaining his right of way.
His case was clear and his will was strong—
But he's as dead as if he'd been wrong.

Mary Ann has gone to rest,
Safe at last on Abraham's breast,
Which may be nice for Mary Ann
But it's certainly rough on Abraham.

Here Skugg lies snug
As a bug in a rug.

In the next five epitaphs the joke is a *pun*, usually on the name of the person. As you read them, try to work out what is meant by the word *pun*.

Ann Mann

Here lies the body of Ann Mann,
Who lived an old woman
But died an old Mann.

Leslie Moore

Here lies what's left
Of Leslie Moore.
No Les,
No more.

A Dentist

Stranger! Approach this spot with gravity!
John Brown is filling his last cavity.

On a Man Named Merideth

Here lies one blown out of breath,
Who lived a merry life, and died a Merideth.

On a Doctor Named Isaac Letsome

When people's ill they comes to I;
I physics, bleeds and sweats 'em.
Sometimes they live, sometimes they die;
What's that to I? I, Letsome.

This epitaph was written for herself by a
woman who always had too much housework.

The Tired Woman's Epitaph

Here lies a poor woman who always was tired
She lived in a house where help was not hired
Her last words on earth were: 'Dear friends, I am going
Where washing ain't done, nor sweeping, nor sewing;
But everything there is exact to my wishes;
For where they don't eat there's no washing of dishes.
I'll be where loud anthems will always be ringing,
But, having no voice, I'll be clear of the singing.
Don't mourn for me now; don't mourn for me never—
I'm going to do nothing for ever and ever.'

Anon.

What is a pun? In which poem is the pun *not*
on the person's name?
What is the pun about in this poem?

The writer Robert Louis Stevenson wrote a serious epitaph for himself, included in this poem:

Requiem

Under the wide and starry sky,
Dig the grave and let me lie.
Glad did I live and gladly die,
And I laid me down with a will.

This be the verse you grave for me:
Here he lies where he longed to be:
Home is the sailor, home from sea,
And the hunter home from the hill.

Robert Louis Stevenson

There are two uses of the word *grave* in this poem. What do they both mean?
Which lines of the poem are the actual epitaph?
Robert Louis Stevenson was a Scottish poet who lived the last part of his life on the island of Samoa in the South Seas. When he wrote *Requiem*, he must have thought that he would return home before he died. But he didn't. He died suddenly and his body is buried on Mount Vaea in Samoa – far from home.

R. L. S. and household on the verandah at Vailima, Samoa

ACTIVITY: **Composing an Epitaph**

Try writing an epitaph poem yourself. Choose someone interesting from history, from fiction or from the news. Compose a few good lines that could be written on that person's gravestone. The poem can be solemn, sad or funny. If it is a funny one, you might be able to work in a pun on the person's name.

Honest Abe

Abraham Lincoln was born in a log cabin in the backwoods of Kentucky in 1809. His parents, Tom and Nancy Hanks Lincoln were very poor indeed. Abraham's childhood was hard, but he fought against his difficulties and grew up to be President of the United States of America. It was Abraham Lincoln who led the Northern States in the American Civil War and the fight against slavery. Abraham Lincoln never forgot his humble beginnings and to many ordinary people he was always known as "Honest Abe". In 1865 he was assassinated – shot dead while watching a play in Ford's Theatre, Washington. These poems tell something of the life of Abraham Lincoln, starting right at the beginning.

Well, Did You Hear?

Well, did you hear? Tom Lincoln's wife today,
The devil's luck for folk as poor as they!
Poor Tom! Poor Nance!
Poor youngun born without a chance!

Edmund Vance Cook

Who do you think is speaking in this poem?
What is the poem trying to say?

Abraham Lincoln's mother, Nancy Hanks Lincoln, died when Abe was very young. The next poem is about her.

Nancy Hanks (1784–1818)

If Nancy Hanks
Came back as a ghost
Seeking news
Of what she loved most,
She'd ask first
"Where's my son?
What's happened to Abe?
What's he done?

"Poor little Abe,
Left all alone
Except for Tom,
Who's a rolling stone;
He was only nine
The year I died
I remember still
How hard he cried.

"Scraping along
In a little shack
With hardly a shirt
To cover his back,
And a prairie wind
To blow him down.
Or pinching times
If he went to town.

"You wouldn't know
About my son?
Did he grow tall?
Did he have fun?
Did he learn to read?
Did he get to town?
Do you know his name?
Did he get on?"

Rosemary and Stephen Benet

Can you answer all Nancy Hanks' questions?

To Meet Mr Lincoln

If I lived at the time
That Mr Lincoln did,
And I met Mr Lincoln
With his stovepipe lid

And his coalblack cape
And his thundercloud beard,
And worn and sad-eyed
He appeared:

"Don't worry, Mr Lincoln,"
I'd reach up and pat his hand,
"We've got a fine President
For this land;

And the Union will be saved,
And the slaves will go free;
And you will live forever
In our nation's memory."

Eve Merriam

What is Mr Lincoln's 'stovepipe lid'? Who do you think is speaking in this poem?
What does the speaker seem to want to do for Mr Lincoln? Why?

In this last poem someone who actually did meet Lincoln remembers him. The speaker is an old man from Maine who was once a soldier in Washington.

A Farmer Remembers Lincoln

'Lincoln?—
Well, I was in the old Second Maine,
The first regiment in Washington from the Pine Tree state.
Of course I didn't get the butt of the clip;
We was there for guardin' Washington—
We was all green.

I ain't never ben to the theayter in my life—
I didn't know how to behave.
I ain't never ben since.
I can see as plain as my hat the box where he sat in
When he was shot.
I can tell you, sir, there was a panic
When we found our President was in the shape he was in!
Never saw a soldier in the world but what liked him.

'Yes, sir. His looks was kind o' hard to forget.
He was a spare man,
An old farmer.
Everything was all right, you know,
But he wasn't a smooth-appearin' man at all—
Not in no ways;
Thin-faced, long-necked,
And a swellin' kind of a thick lip like.

And he was a jolly old fellow—always cheerful;
He wasn't so high but the boys could talk to him their own ways.
While I was servin' at the Hospital
He'd come in and say, 'You look nice in here,'
Praise us up, you know.

And he'd bend over and talk to the boys—
And he'd talk so good to 'em—so close—
That's why I call him a farmer.
I don't mean that everything about him wasn't all right you understand,
It's just—well, I was a farmer—
And he was my neighbor, anybody's neighbor.
I guess even you young folks would 'a' liked him.'

Witter Bynner

What did the old man like about Lincoln?
Does the old man sound like a farmer? Why?
Do you know of any other American Presidents who have been assassinated?

These four poems all need different voices. The last one, for instance, should be read in an old man's voice, slowly, with pauses every now and again as he looks back into his memory. *Nancy Hanks* needs a thin ghost's voice, sad and questioning.
What kind of voices should you use for the other two poems?
Read the poems aloud again with the right tones and expressions. If you like, you can try to read with an American accent.

President Lincoln reviews his soldiers

Mount Rushmore granite sculptures of four U.S. presidents.
Abraham Lincoln is on the left.

ACTIVITY: **Silhouette cutting**

Before cameras were invented, cutting out black paper silhouettes of people in profile (from the side) was a common way of capturing a likeness. You could make a silhouette of Abraham Lincoln who was a very unusual looking man.

Go back through the poems searching for details about his appearance. The picture above is of the gigantic carving of Abraham Lincoln's face on Mount Rushmore in South Dakota, U.S.A. Use it and the details from the unit to give you a good idea of what Lincoln looked like.

1. Draw Lincoln's face in profile on black paper.
2. Add his "stove-pipe" hat.
3. Cut out your silhouette and mount it on white paper.

Conversations

Bird and Boy

So you want to fly. Why?
  You haven't any feathers.
Do you think it's good fun
  Being out in all weathers?
Said Bird to Boy.

You haven't any wings,
  You can't build a nest.
Why aren't you satisfied
  With the things you do best?
Said Bird to Boy.

What would it be like?
  A sky full of boys,
Their arms flapping, their big feet—
  And the noise!
Said Bird to Boy.

Have you ever tried perching
  In some old tree
When it's snowing? It's not funny,
  Believe me!
Said Bird to Boy.

Be comfortable, do your own thing
  Your skateboard, your bike,
Your football, all the other
  Things you like.
    Why try to fly?
  Stay out of the sky,
Said Bird to Boy.

Yes, you're right, I can't just
  Flap my arms and fly.
But I dream about it often,
  Winging through the sky,
Above the houses, the streets.
  I'd like to try.
Said Boy to Bird.

Leslie Norris

Have you ever wanted to be able to fly?
Have you ever dreamt about being able to fly?
Talk about your thoughts and dreams.

Cows

Half the time they munched the grass, and all the time they lay
Down in the water-meadows, the lazy month of May,
　A-chewing,
　A-mooing,
　　To pass the hours away.

"Nice weather," said the brown cow.
　"Ah," said the white.
"Grass is very tasty."
　"Grass is all right."

Half the time they munched the grass, and all the time they lay
Down in the water-meadows, the lazy month of May,
　A-chewing,
　A-mooing,
To pass the hours away.

"Rain coming," said the brown cow.
　"Ah," said the white.
"Flies is very tiresome."
　"Flies bite."

Half the time they munched the grass, and all the time they lay
Down in the water-meadows, the lazy month of May,
　A-chewing,
　A-mooing,
To pass the hours away.

"Time to go," said the brown cow.
　"Ah," said the white.
"Nice chat." "Very pleasant."
　"Night." "Night."

Half the time they munched the grass, and all the time they lay
Down in the water-meadows, the lazy month of May,
    A-chewing,
    A-mooing,
  To pass the hours away.

James Reeves

Do you think this poem should be read quickly
or slowly? *Cows* is a poem which is fun to
read aloud. Try it with two readers being the
cows and the whole class joining in to chant
the chorus.
What sort of voices would be suitable for the
cows?

The next poem is hard to read because part of it is written in nonsense language. This is supposed to be the language spoken by the creatures who live on the planet Mercury. The poem is a conversation between these creatures and the first men to land on Mercury.

To make the poem easier to read, each speech by the Earth men has been marked with an X.

The First Men on Mercury

X – We come in peace from the third planet.
Would you take us to your leader?

– Bawr stretter! Bawr. Bawr. Stretterhawl?

X – This is a little plastic model
of the solar system, with working parts.
You are here and we are there and we
are now here with you, is this clear?

– Gawl horrop. Bawr. Abawrhannahanna!

X – Where we come from is blue and white
with brown, you see we call the brown
here 'land', and blue is 'sea', and the white
is 'clouds' over land and sea, we live
on the surface of the brown land,
all round is sea and clouds. We are 'men'.
Men come—

– Glawp men! Gawrbenner menko. Menhawl?

X – Men come in peace from the third planet
which we call 'earth'. We are earthmen.
Take us earthmen to your leader.

– Thmen? Thmen? Bawr. Bawrhossop.
Yuleeda tan hanna. Harrabost yuleeda.

X – I am the yuleeda. You see my hands,
we carry no benner, we come in peace.
The spaceways are all stretterhawn.

– Glawn peacemen all horrabhanna tantko!
Tan come at'mstrossop.   Glawp yuleeda!

X – Atoms are peacegrawl in our harraban.
Menbat worrabost from tan hannahanna.

– You men we know bawrhossoptant.   Bawr.
We know yuleeda.   Go strawg backspetter quick.

X – We cantantabawr, tantingko backspetter now!

– Banghapper now!   Yes, third planet back.
Yuleeda will go back blue, white, brown
nowhanna!   There is no more talk.

X – Gawl han fasthapper?

– No.   You must go back to your planet.
Go back in peace, take what you have gained
but quickly.

X – Stretterworra gawl, gawl...

– Of course, but nothing is ever the same,
now is it?   You'll remember Mercury.

Edwin Morgan

What happens in this poem?

ACTIVITY: Dramatisation of the First Men on Mercury with sound

1. Divide into groups of six. Two of you are the Earth men, two of you are the Mercurians and two of you are the sound effects team.
2. Earthmen and Mercurians practise reading the poem. It will take some time to become fluent in Mercury talk!
3. Sound effects people sit down with all the sound making equipment you can find and try to work out some good sound effects to go with the poem. You could start with the space ship door shutting and the Earthmen's footsteps and go on from there.
4. Put the reading and the sound effects together and practise the complete presentation.
5. Perform your presentation for the class.

Och Aye, Ee Bah Gum, 'Ow's Yer Farver?

People in different parts of the British Isles have different *accents* or ways of speaking. Sometimes they also have their own special words for things, which strangers to the area do not understand. These words are called *dialect* words.

Poetry often reflects accents and dialects.

The first poem here comes from London. This dialect is called *Cockney*.

Petticoat Lane market, London

Your Biby 'as Fell Dahn the Plug-'Ole

A muvver was barfin' 'er biby one night,
The youngest of ten and a tiny young mite,
The muvver was poor and the biby was thin,
Only a skelington covered in skin;

The muvver turned rahnd for the soap off the rack,
She was but a moment, but when she turned back,
The biby was gorn; and in anguish she cried,
'Oh, where is my biby?'—The angels replied:
'Your biby 'as fell dahn the plug-'ole,
Your biby 'as gorn dahn the plug;
The poor little fing was so skinny and fin
'E oughter been barfed in a jug;
Your biby is perfeckly 'appy,
'E won't need a barf any more,
Your biby 'as fell dahn the plug-'ole,
Not lorst, but gorn before.'

Anon.

Let a few people try saying this poem with a Cockney accent. The spelling should help. Unless you're a Londoner, it may take quite a few tries to get it right.

Next try *Micky Thumps*, a poem from the North of England. This needs an accent similar to the ones on *Coronation Street*.

Micky Thumps

As I was going down Treak Street
For half a pound of treacle,
Who should I meet but my old friend Micky Thumps?
He said to me, 'Wilt thou come to our wake?'
  I thought a bit,
  I thought a bit,
  I said I didn't mind:
  So I went.

As I was sitting on our doorstep
Who should come by but my old friend Micky
Thumps' brother?
He said to me, 'Wilt thou come to our house?
Micky is ill.'
  I thought a bit,
  I thought a bit,
  I said I didn't mind:
  So I went.

And he were ill.
He were gradely ill.
He said to me,
'Wilt thou come to my funeral, man, if I die?'
  I thought a bit,
  I thought a bit,
  I said I didn't mind:
  So I went.

And it were a funeral.
Some stamped on his grave:
Some spat on his grave:
But I scraped my eyes out for my old friend Micky Thumps.

Anon.

Mills in Oldham, Lancashire

What is a *wake* (line 4)?
What do you think *gradely* means?
Do you think this poem is meant to be sad or funny?
Let a few people try saying this poem as someone from the North of England would.
What are some of the differences between this North of England dialect and Cockney?

Scottish farmer's son with pet lamb, around 1900

The next poem is a Scots one, with a number of dialect words. Scottish English is quite different from English English. The poem is about the life of a *dominie*, or village schoolmaster, in the past.
Before trying to read the poem in a Scots accent, read it to yourself and think of what each line means.

The Dominie's Happy Lot

The Dominie is growing grey, 1
  And feth he's keepit thrang
Wi' counts an' spellin' a' the day,
  And liffies when they're wrang.
He dauners out at nine o'clock, 5
  He dauners hame at four—
Frae twal to ane to eat and smoke—
  And sae his day is ower!

Oh! Leezie, Leezie, fine and easy
  Is a job like yon— 10
A' Saturday at gowf to play,
  And aye the pay gaun on!

When winter days are cauld and dark,
  And dykes are deep wi' snaw,
And bairns are shivering' ower their wark, 15
  He shuts the shop at twa;
And when it comes to Hogmanay,
  And fun comes roarin' ben,
And ilka dog maun tak' a day,
  The Dominie tak's ten! 20

Oh! Leezie, Leezie, fine and easy
  Is a job like yon—
To stop the mill whene'er you will,
  And aye the pay gaun on!

And when Inspectors gi'e a ca' 25
  He tak's them roun' to dine,
And aye the upshot o' it a'—
  'The bairns are daein' fine!'

37

And sae the 'Board' come smirkin' roun',
  Wi' prizes in their haun'; 30
And syne it's frae the end o' June
  Until the Lord kens whan!

Oh! Leezie, Leezie, fine and easy
  Is a job like yon—
Sax weeks to jaunt and gallivant, 35
  And aye the pay gaun on!

Walter Wingate

dauners – saunters	*feth* – faith
gaun – going	*ilka* – each
syne – then	*thrang* – busy
frae twal to ane – from twelve to one	*wark* – work
ower – over	*haun'* – hand
Hogmanay – New Year's Eve	*whan* – when
kens – knows	*cauld* – cold
gowf – golf	*snaw* – snow
bairn – child	
ben – into the house	
gallivant – go about idly	
liffies – blows on the hand	

Do you think the dominie had a *happy lot*?
Do you think teachers in general have an easy life?
Let a few people try reading the poem.
Try to read in broad Scots voices.
Why do people in a particular area all have the same accent and know the same dialect words?

ACTIVITY: Accent and Dialect

1. Do you have a local accent in your area? Choose a poem you know quite well from the silver pages or other units in this book and try reading it in your strongest local accent.
2. Do you know any local dialect words which people from another part of the country would not understand? Make a collection of as many as you can. Old people often know lots of dialect words. Ask any old people you know for help.
3. Do you know any poems in your local dialect?
4. In the past, children were often punished for using dialect words in school because teachers believed that dialect wasn't 'good English'. They believed that 'good English' was 'Standard English' – the sort of English people on television often speak. Nowadays many people believe that 'Standard English' is just another dialect, and that all dialects are equally 'good'.
a) Do you understand what 'Standard English' is? Why do you think there is such a thing?
b) Do you ever use 'Standard English'? When? Do you ever use a local dialect? When?
c) Do you think 'Standard English' is better than your local dialect or just different? Why?
d) Can you think of some situations in which it might be more suitable to use your local dialect and some situations in which it might be more suitable to use 'Standard English'?

Glasgow Poets

Dialect poetry is often about trying to catch the special accents and speech habits of one particular community. The poetry in this unit all tries to capture the speech – or ''patter'' – of Glasgow. Tom Leonard and Jimmy Copeland, Margaret Hamilton, Bill Keys, and Stephen Mulrine have all developed a kind of script for the patter, and this really needs to be read aloud. But first of all, you will have to carefully work these poems out for yourself – you have to crack the code, as it were. After a few practice shots, you may then be ready to read them aloud. You may even find you have a natural gift for Glasgow patter!

Try to find a copy of *The Patter: A Guide to Current Glasgow Usage* (by Michael Munro, 1985) in the library if you want to savour more of the delights of Glaswegian speech.

six a clock news

this is thi
six a clock
news thi
man said n
thi reason
a talk wia
BBC accent
iz coz yi
widny wahnt
mi ti talk
aboot thi
trooth wia
voice lik
wanna yoo
scruff. if
a toktaboot
thi trooth
lik wanna yoo
scruff yi

widny thingk
it wuz troo
jist wanna yoo
scruff tokn.
thirza right
way ti spell
ana right way
ti tok it. this
is me tokn yir
right way a
spellin. this
is ma trooth.
yooz doant no
thi trooth
yirsellz cawz
yi canny talk
right. this is
the six a clock
nyooz. belt up.

Tom Leonard

To A' Mice

Two wee mice,
  of the selfsame ilk,   *ilk*: place
Went and fell
  in a bowl of milk.
Ah'm droont!
  the one did drowning utter,
But the other one
  kicked – 'til he stood on butter!

Jimmy Copeland

What is this poem really about? Do you think the six o'clock news should be read in a BBC accent? Why/why not?

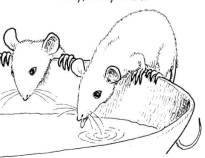

39

A Dug A Dug

Hey, daddy, wid ye get us a dug?
A big broon alsatian ur a wee white pug?
Ur a skinny wee terrier ur a big fat bull?
Aw, daddy, get us a dug. Wull yi?

Whit! An' whose dug'll it be when it durties the flerr,
An' pees'n the carpet, and messes the sterr?
It's me ur yur mammy'll be tane furra mug.
Away oot'n play. Yur no gettin a dug.

But, daddy, thur gien them away
Doon therr at the rspca.
Yu'll get wan fur nothing so yi wull.
Aw, daddy, get us a dug. Wull yi?

Dji hear um? Oan aboot dugs again?
Ah think that yin's goat dugs'n the brain.
Ah know whit yull get: a skite in the lug
If ah hear ony merr aboot this stupid dug.

Ah, daddy, it widny be dear tae keep
An' ah'd make it a basket fur it tae sleep
An' ah'd take it for runs away ower the hull.
Aw, daddy, get us a dug. Wull yi?

Ah doan't think thur's ever been emdy like you:
Yi could wheedle the twist oot a flamin' corkscrew.
Noo! Get doon aff mah neck. Gie's nane a yur hug.
Aw right. That's anuff. Ah'll get yi a dug.

Aw, daddy. A dug. A dug.

Bill Keys

Lament for a Lost Dinner Ticket

See ma mammy
See ma dinner ticket
A pititnma
Pokit an she pititny
Washnmachine.

See thon burnty
Up wherra firewiz
Ma mammy says Am no tellnyagain
No'y playnit.
a just wen'y eatma
Pokacrisps furma dinner
Nabigwoffldoon.

The wummin sed Aver near
Clapsd
Jistur heednur
Wee wellies sticknoot.

They sed Wot heppind?
Nme'nma belly
Na bedna hospital.
A sed A pititnma
Pokit an she pititny
Washnmachine.

They sed Ees thees chaild eb slootly
Non verbal?
A sed MA BUMSAIR
Nwen'y sleep.

Margaret Hamilton

"*thon burnty up wherra firewiz*". The speaker is pointing to a blac
mark on the wall.

A Gude Buke

Ah like a gude buke
a buke's aw ye need
jis settle doon
hiv a right gude read.

Ay, a gude buke's rerr
it makes ye think
nuthin tae beat it
bar a gude drink

Ah like a gude buke
opens yir mine
a gude companion
tae pass the time.

See me wi a buke, bit
in a bus ur a train
canny whack it
wee wurld i yir ain.

Ay, ah like a gude buke
widny deny it
dje know thon wan
noo – whit dje cry it?

Awright, pal, skip it
awright, keep the heid
howm ah tae know
yir tryin tae read?

Stephen Mulrine

Black Friday

Oot behind a lorry,
Peyin nae heed,
Ablow a doubledecker,
A poor wean deid.

Perra worn sannies,
Wee durrty knees,
Heh, erra polis,
Stand back please!

Lookit the conductriss,
Face as white as chalk,
Heh, see the driver, but,
Canny even talk.

Anyone a witness?
Naw, we never saw,
Glad ah'm no' the polis,
Goin' tae tell its maw.

Weemin windae-hingin,
Herts in their mooth,
It's no' oor close, Lizzie,
Oh Gawdstrewth!

Screams on the landin'
Two closes doon,
It's no wee Hughie!
Poor Nellie Broon.

Phone up the shipyard,
Oh, what a shame,
Yes, we'll inform him,
Please repeat the name.

See Big Hughie,
Jokin' wi' the squad,
Better knock aff, Heug,
Oh dear God.

Whit – no' his lauddie?
Aw, bloody hell!
D'ye see Hughie's face but,
He's jist a boy himsel'.

Jimmy Copeland

ablow: below   *sannies*: sandshoes, trainers

Why do you think this poem is best read fairly
quickly – like most of the others in this unit? What
happens if you read them slowly?

The Juniors' Cup Final

The day of the Juniors' Cup Final
Is a day I will never forget,
For the other side's goallie was famous,
He had never let one past him yet!

And on me all my team were dependin',
As the striker to lead the attack,
For our manager said – nae defendin',
Jist get in therr an' nae haudin' back!

From the kick-off I tore down the middle,
An' my wingers baith matched me wi' speed,
Then I passed it oot left frae a dribble,
An' he lobbed – an' I nodded ma heid!

One-Nil – that was just the beginnin',
I knew then the vict'ry was mine,
There was never no doubt who was winnin',
By the half I had nodded in nine!

But I must hand it out to our wingers,
They had that poor goallie near deid,
The pair o' them fair went thir dingers,
When they lobbed – I jist nodded ma heid!

That goallie was full of dejection,
For we kept on increasin' our lead,
He aye dived in the other direction
As I nodded it in with ma heid!

At the whistle that goallie was greetin',
He never had no chance at all,
Twenty goals is how much he was beaten,
All by me and my noddin' the ball!

Well, I met that poor goallie next mornin',
And I hoped he would not make a fuss,
So I gave him a nod in the passin',
And he went and dived under a bus!

Jimmy Copeland

ACTIVITY: **Recitation and dramatisation**
Most of these poems are meant to be funny.
Practise reading them aloud in groups, and see if
you can raise a laugh. You might like to record
some of your better efforts and play them to
another class.

Do you think this kind of writing is suitable for
writing serious poems? Why/why not?

UNIT TEN

Grisly Fates

All the funny poems in this unit are about people who come to sticky ends – usually as a result of their own wickedness. The first one *Matilda* is from *Selected Cautionary Tales For Children* by Hilaire Belloc. A "cautionary tale" is one which is meant to caution or warn the listener how *not* to behave.

Matilda

Matilda told such dreadful lies,
It made one gasp and stretch one's eyes;
Her Aunt, who, from her earliest youth,
Had kept a strict regard for truth,
Attempted to believe Matilda:
The effort very nearly killed her,
And would have done so, had not she
Discovered this infirmity.
For once, towards the close of day,
Matilda, growing tired of play,
And finding she was left alone,
Went tiptoe to the telephone
And summoned the immediate aid
Of London's noble fire-brigade.
Within an hour the gallant band
Were pouring in on every hand,
From Putney, Hackney Downs, and Bow
With courage high and hearts a-glow
They galloped, roaring through the town,
'Matilda's house is burning down!'
Inspired by British cheers and loud
Proceeding from the frenzied crowd,
They ran their ladders through a score
Of windows on the ballroom floor;
And took peculiar pains to souse
The pictures up and down the house,
Until Matilda's Aunt succeeded
In showing them they were not needed;
And even then she had to pay
To get the men to go away!

It happened that a few weeks later
Her Aunt was off to the theatre
To see that interesting play
The Second Mrs Tanqueray,
She had refused to take her niece
To hear this entertaining piece:
A deprivation just and wise
To punish her for telling lies.
That night a fire *did* break out—
You should have heard Matilda shout!
You should have heard her scream and bawl,
And throw the window up and call
To people passing in the street—
(The rapidly increasing heat
Encouraging her to obtain
Their confidence)—but all in vain!
For every time she shouted 'Fire!'
They only answered 'Little liar!'
And therefore when her Aunt returned,
Matilda, and the house, were burned.

Hilaire Belloc

43

Augustus

Augustus was a chubby lad;
Fat, ruddy cheeks Augustus had;
And everybody saw with joy
The plump and hearty, healthy boy.
He ate and drank as he was told,
And never let his soup get cold.

But one day—one cold winter's day,
He screamed out—"Take the soup away!
Oh take the nasty soup away!
I *won't* have any soup to-day."

Next day begins his tale of woes;
Quite lank and lean Augustus grows.
Yet, though he feels so weak and ill,
The naughty fellow cries out still—
"Not any soup for me, I say:
Oh take the nasty soup away!
I *won't* have any soup to-day."

The third day comes: Oh what a sin!
To make himself so pale and thin.
Yet, when the soup is put on table,
He screams, as loud as he is able,
"Not any soup for me, I say:
Oh take the nasty soup away!
I-won't-have-any-soup-to-day."

Look at him, now the fourth day's come!
He scarcely weighs a sugar-plum;
He's like a little bit of thread,
And on the fifth day, he was—dead!

Heinrich Hoffman

The Cruel Naughty Boy

There was a cruel naughty boy,
  Who sat upon the shore,
A-catching little fishes by
  The dozen and the score.

And as they squirmed and wriggled there,
  He shouted loud with glee,
"You surely cannot want to live,
  You're little-er than me."

Just then with a malicious leer,
  And a capacious smile,
Before him from the water deep
  There rose a crocodile.

He eyed the little naughty boy,
  Then heaved a blubbering sigh,
And said, "You cannot want to live,
  You're little-er than I."

The fishes squirm and wriggle still,
  Beside that sandy shore,
The cruel little naughty boy,
  Was never heard of more.

Anon.

44

ACTIVITY 1: **Strip Cartoon Drawing**

1. Choose one of the poems in this unit to make into a comic strip.
2. Read the poem through again carefully and decide how many boxes or "frames" you will need.
3. Use a ruler and a right angle measure of some kind to draw a neat square or rectangle on to card. Cut this out and use it as a template for all your frames.
4. Now draw the action of your poem inside the frames making sure that you make things happen in the right order.
5. You can have bubbles coming out of people's mouths, if you like, inside which you write what people are saying. If you do this, be sure to write the words first and then draw the bubble round them. This way the words always fit!

ACTIVITY 2: **Dramatisation**

The story of Matilda can be made into a play. One person or group of people will be needed to read the poem. Actors will be needed for Matilda, her aunt, the fire brigade and the crowd in the street.

UNIT ELEVEN

Things Are What They Seem

One of the most useful of poetry writing tricks is to be able to make good comparisons. Very often a poet will make a comparison in a poem simply by saying that one thing *is* another. This poem is a good example.

The Toaster

A silver-scaled Dragon with jaws flaming red
Sits at my elbow and toasts my bread.
I hand him fat slices, and then, one by one,
He hands them back when he sees they are done.

William Jay Smith

When a poet says that one thing is another – a toaster is a dragon, for example – he is using a *metaphor*.
What is the metaphor in the next poem?

Steam Shovel

The dinosaurs are not all dead
I saw one raise its iron head
To watch me walking down the road
Beyond our house today.
Its jaws were dripping with a load
Of earth and grass that it had cropped.
It must have heard me where I stopped,
Snorted white steam my way,
And stretched its long neck out to see,
And chewed, and grinned quite amiably.

Charles Malam

In the next poem the poet uses a special sort of metaphor called *personification*.

The Fog

Slowly, the fog,
Hunch-shouldered with a grey face,
Arms wide, advances,
Finger-tips touching the way
Past the dark houses
And dark gardens of roses.
Up the short street from the harbour,
Slowly the fog,
Seeking, seeking;
Arms wide, shoulders hunched,
Searching, searching.
Out through the streets to the fields,
Slowly the fog—
A blind man hunting the moon.

F. R. McCreary

Biographical Notes on Poets

JIMMY COPELAND (1918 –)
Jimmy Copeland's most famous collection is called *The Shoogly Table Book of Verse* (1983). In its introduction, he describes himself modestly as "the greatest Scottish folk-poet now living up his close at Charing Cross, Glasgow, the hub of the known universe."

WALTER DE LA MARE (1873–1956)
Related to Robert Browning. Went to St. Paul's Cathedral Choir School where he started a school magazine. Worked for many years as a clerk. Published first book under pseudonym "Walter Ramal". Became a very famous poet and was awarded the Order of Merit in 1953. The Queen gives this very special honour. Only 24 people can hold it at any one time.

W. W. GIBSON (1878 – 1962)
Born in Northumberland. Educated privately. Wrote from early youth and never had any other job. When he tried to enlist in the 1914–1918 war, he was rejected four times on grounds of bad eye-sight. Eventually accepted in 1917 and served as a private soldier. A poet who wrote of ordinary life and of the scenery of his native Northumberland.

TOM LEONARD (1944 –)
Leonard was born and educated in Glasgow, and he often writes poems in his native diction. At first sight, his language may look incomprehensible and it is not until you read the poems aloud that their meaning begins to emerge. For several years in the 1980s, Tom Leonard worked as Writer in Residence at Paisley Central Library. He lists swimming and snooker as his recreations.

LI PO (707–762)
Born in far west of China. Spent time in his youth as a kind of knight errant – using his sword to help right wrongs. Is said to have killed several men. A very popular poet in his own lifetime. A man with great flashing eyes, a loud voice and a very bad habit of getting drunk. Is said to have died falling drunkenly out of a boat, while trying to catch hold of the reflection of the moon in the water.
N.B. Chinese surnames come first. Li is his surname.

EDWIN MORGAN (1920 –)
Educated in Glasgow. Says, "Ours was not a particularly bookish house. Nor did any of the poetry I learned at school leave a very strong impression on me." All the same, he grew up to write and translate poetry. Taught at Glasgow University. Enjoys photography, keeping scrapbooks and "looking at cities".

PO CHÜ-I (772 – 846)
Lived shortly after Li Po. Father a magistrate but family often short of money. In youth a shy man who found it hard to make friends. Became a very famous poet in later life. Banished by government in 814 for writing poetry which showed sympathy for the poor. Was recalled and later became Governor of Soochow, where he had a lovely time with lots of picnics and feasts. Lived in old age with two cranes for pets and left instructions for a very plain funeral.

JAMES REEVES
A poet, critic, teacher and compiler of anthologies. Has also retold legends, English fairy tales and Bible stories.

Acknowledgements

Thanks are due to the following publishers, agents and authors for permission to reprint the material indicated.

Every effort has been made to trace copyright but if any omissions have been made please let us know in order that we may put it right in the next edition.

George Allen & Unwin Ltd. for 'On His Baldness' trans. by Arthur Waley from *Chinese Poems*.
Angus and Robertson (U.K.) Ltd. for 'The Bunyip' by Douglas Stewart from *Collected Poems 1936 – 37*. Reprinted by permission.
Brandt & Brandt Literary Agents Inc. for 'Nancy Hanks' by Stephen Vincent Benet from *A Book of Americans* by Rosemary & Stephen Vincent Benet © 1933 by R. & S. V. Benet © renewed 1961 by R. Benet. Reprinted by permission.
Jonathan Cape Ltd. for 'I Like a Good Poem' by Roger McGough; 'The Lesson' by Michael Rosen and Roger McGough from *In the Glassroom*; 'Fight of the Year' by Michael Rosen and Roger McGough from *Watchwards*.
Carcanet Press Ltd. for 'The First Men on Mercury' by Edwin Morgan from *Poems of Thirty Years*, Carcanet, Manchester, 1982.
Constable & Co. Ltd. for 'The Lament of Hsi-Chun' trans. by Arthur Waley from *170 Chinese Poems*.
Gerald Duckworth & Co. Ltd. for 'Matilda' by Hilaire Belloc from *Selected Cautionary Tales for Children*.
Harcourt, Brace, Jovanovich Inc. for 'Roast Leviathan' by Louis Untermeyer from *Roast Leviathan*. Copyright 1923, Harcourt, Brace, Jovanovich Inc.; renewed 1951 by Louis Untermeyer. Reprinted by permission of the publisher.
Holt, Rinehart & Winston Publishers for 'Steam Shovel' by Charles Malam from *Upper Pasture*. Copyright 1930, 1958 by Charles Malam. Reprinted by permission.
Nora Hunter for 'Lament for a Lost Dinner Ticket' by Margaret Hamilton.
The Literary Trustees of Walter de la Mare and the Society of Authors as their representative for 'The Listeners' by Walter de la Mare.
James MacGibbon as the Executor of the Estate of Stevie Smith and Allen Lane for 'What Has Happened to Lulu' by Stevie Smith from *The Collected Poems of Stevie Smith*.
Macmillan for 'Flannan Isle' by Wilfred Gibson from *Collected Poems*.
Stephen Mulrine for 'A Gude Buke'. Reprinted by permission.
Leslie Norris for 'Bird and Boy'.

Oxford University Press for 'Cows' by James Reeves. Reprinted from *The Blackbird in the Lilac* by James Reeves, 1952.
Penguin Books Ltd. for 'Quiet Night Thoughts' by Li Po and Tu Fu, trans. by Arthur Cooper (Penguin Classics, 1973) Page 109. Copyright Arthur Cooper, 1973; 'Chivvy' and 'Rodge Said' by Michael Rosen from *You Tell Me*, Puffin, 1981.
R. C. Scriven for 'The Marrog'.
William Jay Smith for 'The Toaster' from *Laughing Time: Nonsense Poems*, Delacorte Press, 1980, © 1955, 1980, William Jay Smith. Reprinted by permission.
The Students' Representative Council of Glasgow University for 'A Dug A Dug' by Bill Keys published in *GUM* 1971.
Cathy Thomson Literary Agent for 'six a clock news' by Tom Leonard. Reprinted by permission.
Franklin Watts Inc. for 'Well, Did You Hear?' by Edmund Vance Cook from *A First Book of Short Verse*.

We are grateful to the following for assistance in providing photographs: British Museum pp. 9 & 10; Freer Gallery of Art, Smithsonian Institute, Washington DC p. 11; Puffin Club, Penguin Books Ltd. pp. 18 & 19; Popperfoto pp. 22 & 35; Mansell Collection pp. 24, 26 & 27; J. Allan Cash Ltd. p. 29; Sefton Photo Library p. 36; National Museum of Antiquities, Country Life Section, Edinburgh p. 37.